Barney Bear, World Traveler

Barney Bear took a trip around the world.

2 **He went to the airport in a taxi**

and over the Pacific Ocean in a plane. 3

4 **He went over the continent on a bus**

and through the mountains in a van. 5

6 He went across the Atlantic Ocean on a ship

and across the country in a train. 7

Barney Bear got back just in time for summer vacation!